You Know You Need a Vacation If...

You Know You Need a Vacation If...

Joey Green and Alan Corcoran

Andrews McMeel Publishing, LLC
Kansas City

For Debbie and Theresa

08 09 10 11 12 WKT 10 9 8 7 6 5 4 3 2 1

ISBN-13: 978-0-7407-7708-0
ISBN-10: 0-7407-7708-4

Library of Congress Control Number: 2008921089

www.andrewsmcmeel.com

Attention: Schools and Businesses

Andrews McMeel books are available at quantity discounts with bulk purchase for educational, business, or sales promotional use. For information, please write to: Special Sales Department, Andrews McMeel Publishing, LLC, 1130 Walnut Street, Kansas City, Missouri 64106.

Introduction

Work, work, work! Back in the 1950s—that glorious decade of tail fins, TV dinners, and time-saving kitchen devices—social scientists began heralding the Age of Leisure (not to be confused with the Age of Aquarius). With swift advances in productivity, efficiency, and golf technology around the corner, Americans were advised to get ready for an extended period of serious goofing off. Production was stepped up on badminton sets, backyard barbecues, and 3-D glasses.

But a funny thing happened on the way to the three-day workweek. Increased efficiency led to downsizing, rightsizing, supersizing, and an ocean of pink slips. "Cradle-to-grave employment" was replaced by "early retirement." Those spared the ax were told to carry the load of their departed brethren, join them in line at the unemployment office, or start up their own Internet company. The drumbeat of global competition grew louder and louder: *Lower Prices! Higher Quality! Got Milk?*

Letters gave way to faxes. Four-to-six weeks shipping shrank to "Next day!" Telephones invaded our cars, our planes, and our bathrooms. Pagers tracked us down and e-mail finished us off. There was nowhere to run and nowhere to hide.

The result of this new, improved, turbocharged Work Ethic? A gargantuan National Sleep Deficit and skyrocketing Public Stress Levels. Work place shootings have migrated from the post office to the home office. People work all day at the office, work all night at home, and—when they can't stand it anymore—they take a working vacation. If they gain the world and lose their soul in the process, at least it's a tax deduction.

The time has come to reverse this destructive trend. We must declare war on the disease of hyperefficiency and reembrace the American virtues of laziness, indolence, and sloth. Take a vacation! Rejuvenate your soul! Stop and smell the roses! Workers of the world unite! You have nothing to lose but your health insurance.

But before you start working overtime to plan that vacation, you must first admit that you have a problem. And so, as a public service, we've prepared the following checklist—to help you determine whether your job has taken over your life—in case you've been working too hard to notice.

You Know
You Need
a Vacation
If...

You dial 9
for an outside line—
from home.

Your dog attacked you when you came home from an extended road trip.

● ● ● ● ●

You listened to your son's graduation speech on your cell phone.

Your favorite TV program is the CNN airport news.

● ● ● ● ●

The longest vacation you had this year was when a Chicago snowstorm forced you to stay overnight at the O'Hare Sheraton.

You have the numbers of the top three all-night pizza delivery places programmed into your speed dial.

You've pulled three all-nighters this week and it's only Tuesday.

You pick up the kids at school, drive them to soccer practice, dance rehearsal, piano lessons, and religious school, go to the McDonald's drive-through for dinner, get home in time to do the laundry and get the kids to bed—only to discover that your spouse has the audacity to try to seduce you.

You've paid $35 for missing a dentist appointment.

● ● ● ● ●

You can eat an Egg McMuffin, talk on the phone, apply eye makeup, and read a newspaper while driving seventy miles-per-hour on the freeway.

Instead of having your dentist pull out all your wisdom teeth at once, you decided to have one wisdom tooth extracted each month—because you consider a trip to the dentist rest and relaxation.

You explained the "birds and the bees" to your child–via e-mail.

• • • • •

Your exercise program consists of purchasing really expensive home gym equipment and then making room for it in your garage.

You've got items on your To Do list that date back to the Reagan administration.

People tell you to "work smarter, not harder" in your dreams.

You can fit two suits, five shirts, a pair of shoes, socks, underwear, ties, and toiletries into a carry-on bag the size of a shoebox.

● ● ● ● ●

You were caught in a compromising position with your computer mouse.

You RSVP to weddings and bar mitzvahs six months after they've taken place.

• • • • •

You have experienced the pain and humiliation of "keyboard face."

You get nervous any time your daily new e-mail count drops below thirty.

• • • • •

You have enough frequent-flier miles to earn a seat on the board of directors of three major airlines.

When your office received the team picture of the soccer squad you sponsored, you weren't sure which player was your daughter.

You have $5,000 worth of titanium golf clubs that you used once—to take a lesson.

● ● ● ● ●

You have no trouble addressing 10,000 shareholders, but you break into a sweat at the prospect of a parent-teacher conference.

There's half of a
tuna fish sandwich
on a kaiser roll
in your out-box.

You delete office e-mail jokes without reading them.

● ● ● ● ●

Even though you wear a Bluetooth headset twenty-four hours a day, you don't have time to call your mother.

You own a postal scale that lists postage prices from three postal hikes ago.

There's a pillow and blanket in the bottom drawer of your file cabinet.

You haven't had time to read *The One-Minute Manager*.

You ask colleagues to accompany you to the restroom to use that time as a business meeting.

Your lunch today was a Three Musketeers bar.

• • • • •

You've burnt out the alternator in your car engine because you didn't have time to check the oil.

If caffeinated beverages
were made illegal, you'd be
in a methadone clinic.

● ● ● ● ●

You carry a cell phone and
a pager and still check your
voice mail every five minutes.

21

You've sent a fax through an air phone.

● ● ● ● ●

The only movies you see are on business flights—but never with the headset.

You use your cell phone to make calls from your driveway.

● ● ● ● ●

The only surfing you do is on the Internet.

You consider a paper jam in the photocopier equivalent to a nuclear meltdown.

You have a brand-new Brooks Brothers shirt in the bottom drawer of your office desk.

You set your wristwatch ten minutes fast and you're still ten minutes late to meetings.

You're convinced traffic jams are a cosmic conspiracy plotted specifically against you.

● ● ● ● ●

You get into the office at 7 a.m. to get more work done, but fail to complete it by 7 p.m.

You've had a can of Coca-Cola for breakfast.

If people don't return your phone calls within twenty minutes, you scratch them off your Christmas card list.

You treat telemarketers
like mosquitoes.

• • • • •

**You think if you take
a vacation, the entire
infrastructure of your
company will collapse.**

The papers in your in-box could fill three shopping bags.

● ● ● ● ●

You've instructed your secretary to buy a gift for herself for National Secretary Day.

Your most exciting hobbies are paying the bills, doing your taxes, and throwing away junk mail.

• • • • •

You tailgate slow-moving vehicles for thrills.

You stay five hours late at the office "to avoid rush-hour traffic."

You're convinced
that handicapped
parking spaces include
people in a hurry.

You give your loved one the same Valentine's Day card every year.

● ● ● ● ●

In the event of an emergency, you could live off the food stuck in your laptop computer for three days.

The only church you attend is in turbulence at 35,000 feet.

• • • • •

You send Christmas presents via FedEx Priority Overnight.

You go grocery shopping at two in the morning to avoid the crowds and buy only canned ravioli, Lean Cuisine microwaveable TV dinners, and a twelve pack of Mountain Dew.

You remember to change the kitty litter only after your cat leaves a present for you on the carpet.

You think office birthday parties impede productivity but the cake provides a welcome sugar rush.

Every meal you've had in the last month was a business lunch.

● ● ● ● ●

The only sex you get is five sample minutes of the Adult Channel in business hotel rooms.

The only newspaper you see is a complimentary copy of *USA Today* and you only skim the front page.

● ● ● ● ●

You've brought a box of assorted Dunkin' Donuts into work in the hopes your colleagues will overlook the fact that you're an hour late.

The last time you had dinner at the same table with your family was Thanksgiving.

You fell asleep in the movie theater during *Saving Private Ryan*.

39

If an item at the supermarket requires a price check at the cash register, you cancel your entire order and leave the store.

● ● ● ● ●

When airport security officers insist upon searching your luggage, you insist you don't have time.

Your briefcase contains three backup batteries for your cell phone.

• • • • •

You haven't seen the floor of your office in three months.

• • • • •

You've returned unwatched DVDs to Blockbuster three months late.

You've never changed the incoming message on your answering machine.

• • • • •

You've spent an entire morning going from call-waiting call to call-waiting call to call-waiting call.

You can't understand why anyone would waste their time watching the Academy Awards when they can read the winners the next morning.

● ● ● ● ●

A book entitled *How to Get Rid of Clutter* is buried somewhere on your desk.

Your dry cleaner invited you to his daughter's wedding.

• • • • •

More than half the pens in your pencil holder don't write.

• • • • •

You own stock in Post-it notes.

The floor on the passenger side of your car looks like the trash bin at McDonald's.

To get away from the office, you go to Staples or CompUSA.

45

You've been reading the same novel for the last three years.

• • • • •

You've taken your laptop computer and cell phone to the beach.

• • • • •

The graveyard-shift custodian is one of your closest friends.

You've raced to the door at the post office to get in line before an old lady using a walker.

• • • • •

You fell asleep on your bed fully dressed, and the next morning, you went to work in the exact same clothes.

You have a framed picture of
Ayn Rand on your desk.

• • • • •

**You've postponed a dental
appointment more than three times.**

• • • • •

You don't have time for a
time management seminar.

"If you want something done right, do it yourself" is tattooed on your forehead.

You rotate your tires more often than you change the sheets on your bed.

You hold Power Breakfasts, eat Power Bars, and give Power handshakes.

● ● ● ● ●

You keep a micro-recorder on your night table.

You're convinced that losing your Filo-Fax would result in the fall of Western civilization.

● ● ● ● ●

You use a speakerphone so you can continue shining your shoes with a Wash 'n Dri.

You only use gas pumps
that accept credit cards.

• • • • •

You keep papers and books
on all the chairs in your
office to prevent other
people from sitting down and
wasting your valuable time.

You finish other people's sentences for them.

• • • • •

You consider "Taking Care of Business" your personal theme song.

• • • • •

You send Christmas cards via the Internet.

The only time you get to do yoga exercises is while waiting for elevators.

You return phone calls during the lunch hours in each time zone so you don't have to talk to anyone.

You've noticed that by the time you finish entering all your contacts and phone numbers into a personal digital assistant, a new generation has come along and you have to start all over again.

You get a tingly feeling all over whenever you go to an office supply store.

Your voice mail message says "I'll return your call when it's convenient or when hell freezes over—whichever comes first."

You bought an annual pass to Disneyland and never made it to the park before it expired.

There's a bag of merchandise in the trunk of your car that you've been meaning to return to Home Depot since last summer.

You've searched the grocery store shelves for something stronger than Jolt.

• • • • •

You don't mind paying $3.50 for a double espresso at Starbucks because "it's still cheaper than crystal meth."

You bought a special TV tuner card for your PC so you could watch the Super Bowl while you printed W2 forms.

● ● ● ● ●

You waste hundreds of hours every year trying to use time-saving devices.

You've trimmed your toenails in the back of a cab on the way to the airport.

• • • • •

You have 26 gigabytes worth of important data on your PC and a 600 GB backup system you've never used.

You pulled out your back installing
a twenty-five-inch monitor
you bought to compensate
for your failing eyesight.

• • • • •

You've got an office at work,
an office at home, and an
office in the bathroom.

You wear a lead-lined hat on plane trips to reduce your annual radiation exposure.

• • • • •

You've been assigned your own private FedEx guy.

Your Hilton VIP card says "Whatever metal that's more precious than platinum."

Your travel agent gave you
a new car for Christmas.

Your fantasies include hiring the Mafia to collect your accounts receivable.

You wish they allowed Rollerblades at trade shows.

You attended the office Christmas party via videoconferencing.

• • • • •

You have a reserved parking space at Kinko's.

You found a dentist located next to a barbershop so you can have your hair cut and your teeth cleaned at the same time.

• • • •

You had a heliport built in your backyard to cut twenty minutes off your office commute.

You read *The Seven Habits of Highly Effective People* three times and can't remember a single one of them.

● ● ● ● ●

The time and energy required to find a lower mortgage would actually cost you money.

Your notebook computer bag contains electrical cords for twenty-seven countries on four different continents.

You hand a shoebox filled with receipts to the guy at H&R Block and agree to pay whatever it costs to do your taxes.

You know the aisle number for the exit rows on a 737, 747, 757, 767, MD80, MD11, and a Fokker 100.

You can no longer read your own handwriting.

• • • • •

You know ten foolproof ways to get out of jury duty.

• • • • •

You consider the salad bar at Denny's a gourmet meal.

You don't have time to see a doctor about your ulcer.

● ● ● ● ●

Your dishwasher doubles
as the china cabinet.

● ● ● ● ●

You've gone into the office with double pneumonia.

What Other People Say About Work

"If *A* is a success in life, then *A* equals
x plus *y* plus *z*. Work is *x*; *y* is play; and
z is keeping your mouth shut."
—*Albert Einstein*

"If you don't want to work, you have to work to earn enough money so that you won't have to work."
—*Ogden Nash*

•

"One of the symptoms of an approaching nervous breakdown is the belief that one's work is terribly important, and that to take a holiday would bring all kinds of disaster. If I were a medical man, I should prescribe a holiday to any patient who considered his work important."
—*Bertrand Russell*

"When you see what some girls marry, you realize how they must hate to work for a living."
—*Helen Rowland*

•

"Anyone can do any amount of work provided it isn't the work he is supposed to be doing at that moment."
—*Robert Benchley*

•

"My father taught me to work, but not to love it. I never did like to work, and I don't deny it. I'd rather read, tell stories, crack jokes, talk, laugh—anything but work."
—*Abraham Lincoln*

"Genius is 1 percent inspiration
and 99 percent perspiration."
–Thomas Edison

•

"All work and no play makes Jack a dull boy."
–James Howell

•

"Work is the refuge of people who
have nothing better to do."
–Oscar Wilde

•

"Work as if you were to live a hundred years,
Pray as if you were to die tomorrow."
–Benjamin Franklin

"I go on working for the same reason
that a hen goes on laying eggs."
−*H. L. Mencken*

•

"Man may work from sun to sun,
But woman's work is never done."
−*Anonymous*

•

"They intoxicate themselves with work
so they won't see how they really are."
−*Aldous Huxley*

You yearn for the time when you paid to attend six hours of lectures a day and had twelve weeks to read nineteen textbooks, write four research papers, and take six final exams.

• • • • •

You have no idea what your house looks like in the daylight.

You've taken a laptop computer on a ski lift.

You see the inherent beauty in a sea of illuminated red brake lights on the interstate.

Your definition of a vacation is when you check your e-mail and voice mail only twice a day.

You've learned to shave in severe turbulence without opening any major arteries.

The odometer on your laser printer has gone over 1 million pages.

• • • • •

The last live concert you attended featured Buddy Holly, Ritchie Valens, and the Big Bopper.

Your Club Med membership
has been revoked.

●　●　●　●　●

**You wear a cordless headset
so you won't miss calls when
you're in the bathroom.**

You met your spouse online
and hope one day you'll have
time to meet her in person.

• • • • •

You have a secret addiction
to the fumes generated by
erasable whiteboard markers.

You've plucked your eyebrows while waiting at a subway station.

• • • • •

You have voted by absentee ballot in every election since Dukakis.

• • • • •

You consider mankind's greatest invention to be the binder clip.

You know the precise locations and quitting times of all employees with snacks stashed in their cubicles.

You have a dozen empty bottles of Visine in your top desk drawer.

You have a laminated name tag in the pocket of every jacket you own.

• • • • •

All of your business letters end with the phrase "dictated but not signed."

• • • • •

You talk in shorthand.

You shower and shave at the gym,
but never have time to work out.

• • • • •

**You still have a box of 4.5-inch
floppy disks on your shelf.**

• • • • •

You own five Berlitz books
that you've never used.

86

You had a conference call to discuss your child's report card with the teacher and your spouse.

● ● ● ● ●

You've single-handedly billed a client 720 hours in one week.

You have a personal shredder
in the backseat of your car.

● ● ● ● ●

**You don't own any
casual clothes.**

● ● ● ● ●

**You consider maternity leave
the same thing as retirement.**

Your secretary "forgot" to put more than ten appointments on your calendar this week.

• • • • •

The only time you call the customer service number for your credit card is after 2 a.m.

The American Dream has become your own personal nightmare.

Every phone call you make is interrupted by three other phone calls.

When asked, "Is it all right if I put you on hold?," you reply, "Definitely not."

When you finally get an hour to yourself, you have no idea how to relax.

You've used your fax machine to copy
a three-hundred-page document.

• • • • •

**You refer to your car
as your office.**

• • • • •

You've asked the mailroom guy to
run out and buy some Dexatrim.

You've been asked to drop everything and take on a more crucial project three times this week.

● ● ● ● ●

Your significant other is a Macy's lingerie ad.

Your new passport photo
looks like Chewbacca.

For relaxation, you read the
mail-order catalog from a
computer warehouse.

You made an appointment
to see Dr. Kevorkian.

**You keep a toothbrush, tube
of toothpaste, and a stick of
roll-on deodorant in the top
drawer of your file cabinet.**

Your luggage has twice as much frequent-flyer mileage as you do.

• • • • •

A palm reader offered to refund your money.

• • • • •

Your dog is suing you for neglect.

Your dirty laundry is threatening
to become nuclear waste.

• • • • •

**You accidentally sent your
car payment to the IRS.**

• • • • •

Your checkbook makes the
federal budget look balanced.

97

You locked your keys in your car while the motor was running.

● ● ● ● ●

You received three birthday cards—all addressed "Resident."

● ● ● ● ●

You haven't turned the page on your wall calendar since October 1997.

The mildew in your shower spoke to you.

You ignore all fire alarms
and refuse to stop working
until you see flames.

You broke your arm trying to stop an elevator door from closing.

You keep a gas-powered electrical generator and a carton of provisions in your office—just in case.

100

A vase of dead roses has been sitting in your office for the past two years.

● ● ● ● ●

You haven't filled out a time sheet since Labor Day.

● ● ● ● ●

You didn't notice that your spouse left you three weeks ago.

You enjoy working weekends because there's less traffic, no distracting phone calls, and plenty of space in the conference room for a picnic.

You ate pizza at your desk on Easter Sunday.

• • • • •

The rubber plant in the conference room is suing you for sexual harassment.

Your garbage cans have sat out on the curb for an entire week.

• • • • •

You consider "Oh, thank heaven for 7-Eleven" a psalm.

• • • • •

Your clean clothes sit at the foot of your dresser in a laundry basket.

Half the lightbulbs in your house are dead.

● ● ● ● ●

You've worn the same underwear three days in a row.

● ● ● ● ●

The timer on your sprinkler system is still set on daylight saving time.

105

You've forgotten your best friend's first name.

You long for the day when you'll have time to sharpen all your pencils in your electric pencil sharpener.

You've been caught naked
in the supply closet.

**You consider a bag of
microwave popcorn "dinner"
and a coffee filter "fine china."**

**You've heard yourself say,
"Get to the punch line."**

• • • • •

You've never made it to a
company softball game—
and you're the captain.

Your entire reason for living can be summed up in two words: corner office.

● ● ● ● ●

You look forward to being assigned projects on Friday afternoon at five.

When you listen for your inner voice, you hear the roar of a leaf blower.

You know how to ask "Where is the restroom?" with a perfect accent in seven languages.

You don't have time to
live in the present.

• • • • •

**You can sleep standing up
on a crowded subway.**

• • • • •

Your checkbook register
doubles as your diary.

You have a "home" toothbrush and an "away" toothbrush.

You've surreptitiously called your own beeper with the speed-dial button on your cell phone to excuse yourself from a meeting.

112

You know precisely how many days you can live on Swiss Miss instant hot chocolate, Cup O'Noodle soup, and sugar packets before the really bad hallucinations kick in.

You've canceled appointments with people sitting in the waiting room.

You've applied nail polish while working out on a StairMaster.

• • • • •

You can decide in the first three seconds whether to listen to, save, delete, or forward a voice mail message.

Your office is wallpapered with pink "While You Were Out" slips.

• • • • •

You can arrange your luggage in front of a seat at the airport gate to create a makeshift twin bed.

Your administrative aide has
an administrative aide.

• • • • •

**You introduced your fiancé
to your parents using
three-way calling.**

• • • • •

You see a three-day weekend as a
chance to get more work done.

Your doctor diagnosed your eating disorder by analyzing the contents of your computer keyboard.

● ● ● ● ●

Every book you read last year was written for Dummies or Idiots.

You think Dilbert has a pretty good gig with a pretty sharp outfit.

● ● ● ● ●

Your cubicle has been declared a biohazard.

● ● ● ● ●

You developed carpal tunnel syndrome from dialing the phone.

You maxed out your Social Security deduction before Groundhog Day.

•　•　•　•　•

You check your e-mail in the car on the way into the office.

•　•　•　•

You've thanked God for the Sharpie fine-point permanent marker.

You live your life according to the principles espoused in *The One-Minute Manager, The One-Minute Employee*, and *The One-Minute Lover*.

You will have to live to be 140 to complete all of the To Do items in your personal information manager.

● ● ● ● ●

You've snuck out of church services to take a business call on your vibrating cell phone.

You consider a trip through the Burger King drive-through a way of pampering yourself.

You upgraded your Blackberry to improve your view of your baby's first steps.

The Cub Scout troop you run has a mission statement.

• • • • •

You have a reminder on Microsoft Office Outlook to clip your toenails.

• • • • •

You refer to your employees as "my people."

For relaxation, you've alphabetized all your books, CDs, and DVDs.

● ● ● ● ●

You know exactly where to buy the 3.3-ounce size of anything.

● ● ● ● ●

The last time you wore a bathing suit, it had stripes and sleeves.

If you cash in your unused, paid time off, the company will be forced to sell off its financial services division.

The police arrested you for stalking, but they dropped the charges when your kids recognized you.

Technically you're not a vampire, but you're still afraid to risk sunlight exposure.

The last time you went to Disneyland, the price of admission was less than twenty bucks.

● ● ● ● ●

You've used "I had a dentist appointment" three times this year to explain why you were out of the office.

You Know You Need a Vacation If . . .

You were relieved to find a Workaholics Anonymous group that meets in your building.

You instructed your aide to call a car service for your wife when she went into labor.

128

You rang up a euphoria-induced, $500 cell-phone bill when you discovered that you could use your Razr to call your New York office from Paris, France.

You paid the airline an extra ten bucks to guarantee that your adjacent seatmates had bathed within the last twenty-four hours.

129

You gave your laptop a name and sleep with it under your pillow.

●　●　●　●　●

You sleep under your desk to cut down on the commute.

●　●　●　●　●

You called your Blackberry from your cell phone just to check in.

130

You had to wear a "Clapton is God" T-shirt to a Japanese business meeting when the airline lost your luggage and you lost your wallet.

• • • • •

You were sent to a rehab clinic by the head barista at Starbucks after a weeklong espresso bender.

You pooled your company's phone sex and suicide hotline operators to streamline operations.

• • • • •

You accidentally mixed up your Viagra and Xanax and had to stay behind your desk all day.

132

You forgot to show up for commitment counseling.

• • • • •

You experienced a very confusing weekend at the Forty-sixth Annual Hooker's Convention.

The cleaning crew gives you a once-over with the Hoover when they come through at night.

You've scheduled meetings just so you could get some doughnuts.

You've developed an unhealthy relationship with the office supplies.

You can tell how old you are by counting the rings in your coffee cup.

On weekends during the summer, your spouse gets a conjugal visit at your office.

• • • • •

You finally showed up to have your teeth cleaned only to discover that your dentist died two years ago.

You check your kids' homework on MySpace.

• • • • •

The Guinness Book of Records lists you as the world's oldest person based on your billed hours.

137

You accidentally milked
the chickens and harvested
the cow's eggs.

• • • • •

You fired someone just
to lift your mood.

You inadvertently sent out a memo declaring the last day of the week "Casual Sex Friday."

• • • • •

You created a thirty-two-slide PowerPoint presentation on how to make PowerPoint presentations more interesting.

You were busted using the Cray 950 supercomputer to determine fantasy football draft picks.

● ● ● ● ●

After using Gmail, instant messaging, MySpace, stock trades, Yahoo news, YouTube, and iTunes, you only have about ten minutes a day to get any real work done.

You had to give up
telecommuting when
your colleagues
complained they
couldn't hear
the conference
call over
Judge Judy.

The Secret of Success

"If you think nobody cares if you're alive, try missing a couple of car payments."
—*Flip Wilson*

"The secret of life is honesty and fair dealing. If you can fake that, you've got it made."
—*Groucho Marx*

•

"Let a smile be your umbrella, and you'll end up with a face full of rain."
—*George Carlin*

•

"The secret of staying young is to live honestly, eat slowly, and lie about your age."
—*Lucille Ball*

"The only really happy folk are married women and single men."
—*H. L. Mencken*

•

"The two most beautiful words in the English language are: 'check enclosed.'"
—*Dorothy Parker*

•

"Bisexuality immediately doubles your chances for a date on Saturday night."
—*Woody Allen*

"Too much of a good thing is wonderful."
—*Mae West*

•

"If life was fair, Elvis would be alive and all the impersonators would be dead."
—*Johnny Carson*

•

"Pleasure in the job puts perfection in the work."
—*Aristotle*

•

"Let us be thankful for the fools. But for them the rest of us could not succeed."
—*Mark Twain*

You cried on the inside when you found out that the "Greatest Boss Ever" mug was a gag gift.

• • • • •

You attracted the wrong kind of attention when you declared, "Every Day is Bring Your Daughters to Work Day."

You've pulled three all-nighters in a row.

● ● ● ● ●

The proudest day of your life was successfully forwarding a telephone call to someone else's voice mail—without hanging up on the caller.

You attach tiny Post-it notes to oversized Post-it notes.

● ● ● ● ●

You've prerecorded videotaped birthday greetings to be played in your inevitable absence.

You've had recurring nightmares where you are trapped for days by a blizzard at the Denver Airport.

• • • • •

You've woken up from that same nightmare, relieved to discover you are still safely stranded by thunderstorms at the Dallas/Fort Worth Airport.

Every day you try to eat from the four basic food groups: takeout, delivery, drive-through, and airplane.

Your in-box is made of reinforced concrete.

● ● ● ● ●

Your cell-phone bill comes in a crate.

● ● ● ● ●

Your mantra is "I don't have time for this crap."

You've had a heart-to-heart conversation with the Romanian woman who empties the wastepaper basket in your office at 2 a.m.

You've written six research papers, read sixteen novels, and highlighted an entire biology textbook in the last twenty-four hours.

You enthusiastically participate in conference calls while sitting on the toilet.

Your refrigerator contains a bottle of ketchup, a jar of mustard, a carton of rotting Kung Pao chicken, and a Rubbermaid container that now qualifies as a petri dish.

153

The pile of mail stacked up on the table in the front hallway contains at least six envelopes stamped "final notice."

● ● ● ● ●

You don't have time to sort through all of your pens to toss out the ones that don't work.

You've driven to three different post offices to avoid standing in the long line at any of them.

● ● ● ● ●

Your newsboy might as well toss your daily newspaper directly into your trash bin.

The water in your pool looks like pea soup.

● ● ● ● ●

You've gotten an extension on the extension on your taxes.

● ● ● ● ●

You send out your Christmas cards on Martin Luther King's birthday.

Netflix is threatening to repossess your DVD player.

• • • • •

You submitted your college applications overnight via Express Mail.

• • • • •

Your personal trainer has no idea what you look like.

The last six movies you saw were on a thirteen-inch tube suspended from the middle aisle of a 757.

You've considered outsourcing foreplay to improve efficiency.

Your multitasking combines a conference call, a haircut, and a bathroom break.

Your entire vocabulary consists of "touching base," "being on the same page," and "singing to the choir."

You know all the wireless hotspots between LGA and JFK.

• • • • •

You can ask for No-Doz in thirteen European languages and three Chinese dialects.

You can explain, on a city-by-city basis, how daylight saving time works in Indiana and Arizona.

● ● ● ● ●

You've actually sharpened your pencils to the point where they are too short to fit in the sharpener.

You crossed a French modem adapter with a Brazilian phone charger to power your laptop in Ghana.

● ● ● ● ●

You've googled Ted Kaczynski for tips on reducing your monthly expenses.

You've brushed your teeth, trimmed your fingernails, and waxed your back on your way in to work.

• • • • •

You know thirty-seven tasty and nutritious combinations of rice and beans.

Your retirement portfolio is heavily weighted in Beanie Babies.

● ● ● ● ●

You check your voicemail during sex.

● ● ● ● ●

You're a member of the million mocha club at Starbucks.

You accidentally posted your résumé on eBay.

• • • • •

Your cubicle is the birthplace of Christian Rap Jazz Country Fusion.

• • • • •

Your kid's day care program is picking strawberries.

You've got plane tickets to six different countries on three continents in your underwear drawer.

You mixed blue food coloring in your jar of peanut butter to catch the office freegan.

Your ability to juggle cash advances, minimum payments, and interest-free transfers have attracted the attention of three South American finance ministers.

You were banned from Best Buy after your third post–Super Bowl HDTV return.

You'd sleep like a baby every night–if you didn't have one.

● ● ● ● ●

Your supervisor at Wal-Mart caught you moonlighting at Costco.

● ● ● ● ●

Your e-mail in-box takes twenty minutes to load.

You gave up your cushy job at the laundry for the fast-paced world of poultry processing.

● ● ● ● ●

You organized a strike when a health-conscious assistant manager replaced the M&M's in the break room vending machine with carrot sticks.

You got docked for time spent talking to a suicide counselor.

● ● ● ● ●

Your new company fitness program: human-size hamster wheels.

● ● ● ● ●

Al Gore estimates your commute is raising global temperatures.

You don't take down your Christmas lights until July Fourth, at which point, you seriously consider leaving them up for the rest of the year.

To cut costs, your boss replaced the coffeemaker in the break room with a Taser.

• • • • •

You're honestly interested in hearing the Windows shortcuts shared by the computer guy while he's using the adjacent urinal.

CSI matched your ass to the butt-print left on the photocopier glass.

• • • • •

The boss found lurid photos of Tinky Winky on your office computer.

• • • • •

Your new boss replaced Casual Friday with White Tie Wednesdays.

173

The IRS taxed you on the fair market value of your employee-of-the-week parking space.

• • • • •

The human resources department gave you a choice between "Lackey," "Flunky," or "Sycophant" for your business cards.

Your company's disaster recovery plan is "Take the money and run."

You were caught revealing the eleven secret herbs and spices in an FBI sting operation.

You've accrued enough vacation days to travel to another galaxy.

● ● ● ● ●

You've worn the letters off your computer keyboard.

● ● ● ● ●

Mom is Chairman of the Board; you're Disappointment-in-Chief.

You haven't taken a vacation in the last ten years and you brag about it.

● ● ● ● ●

You came down with a severe case of the flu, washed down a handful of Sudafed with a six-pack of Red Bull, and went into work anyway.

TiVo recorded a three-day *Law and Order* marathon and you can't find the time to delete all seventy-two episodes.

• • • • •

You seriously considered sending out your wedding invitations as an e-mail blast.

You've got envelopes of developed photographs hidden in closets, bookshelves, and drawers throughout your home, and you stand a better chance of winning the lottery than ever putting those photographs into albums in chronological order.

You've driven sixty miles-per-hour, weaving recklessly in and out of traffic, only to end up waiting at a red light along with every other car you passed.

You've been nearly crushed to death by closing subway doors.

Every time you've tried to go the bathroom for the last ten years, one of your kids walks in.

You left your briefcase, laptop computer, and a large cup of coffee on the roof of your car—all in the same day.

Your financial advisor recommends you retire three to four years after your death.

● ● ● ● ●

You don't have time to flip through every channel to see if there's anything on TV.

You forgot to set your clocks back an hour, but it didn't affect your life whatsoever.

● ● ● ● ●

You've come to the awful realization that what goes up will inevitably come back down and hit you in the head.

183

You've been running two hours late for the last six years.

● ● ● ● ●

Your weekend runs from 11 p.m. Saturday to 5 a.m. Sunday.

● ● ● ● ●

You get most of your work done at the laundromat.

Hors d'oeuvres at happy hour are your version of a four-course dinner.

● ● ● ● ●

Your apartment is nothing more than a glorified changing room.

● ● ● ● ●

The only exercise you get is running up the escalator two steps at a time.

You've just been promoted to the Department of Unknown Unknowns.

● ● ● ● ●

You've slammed the door on a ten-year-old Girl Scout selling cookies.

● ● ● ● ●

You consider a week on jury duty the equivalent of a trip to Hawaii.

You secretly wish that sitting around all day in your pajamas watching *Dr. Phil* was a legitimate career path.

● ● ● ● ●

You've discovered that the best way to get a table at a restaurant is to bring your own.

You call most of your co-workers "friend," "buddy," or "pal," because you're too busy to memorize their names.

• • • • •

You've discovered that leaving your dirty dishes in the sink doesn't necessarily mean that someone else will wash them.

You don't have time to ponder whether the glass is half empty or half full.

• • • • •

You haven't cleaned out your glove compartment since the day you bought the car.

If someone offers you a tic tac, you jump to the conclusion that they're really suggesting Listerine.

When the waitress at a restaurant starts reciting the day's specials, you cut her off with the words, "We're ready to order."

190

You were upset to learn that it takes more than a minute to make Minute Rice.

You've had a romantic conversation on your cell phone while walking across a parking lot searching for your car.

You've put people on hold in the hopes that they'd eventually hang up and never call back.

● ● ● ● ●

You joined Workaholics Anonymous and got three job offers at the first meeting.

You've willingly paid the erroneous $35 fee on your checking account statement rather than spend an hour on the phone trying to straighten out the mistake.

You're haunted by the thought that keeping your nose to the grindstone will turn you into Michael Jackson.

● ● ● ● ●

You're getting a full eight hours of sleep—as long as you count your commute.

When your spouse said, "You need to recharge your batteries," you plugged in your cell phone.

● ● ● ● ●

You've pulled into the parking garage at work without any recollection of having driven there.

Your philosophy: The light at the end of the tunnel is just another train heading straight at you.

Your career goal is to be promoted to a position in the orphan's workhouse in Charles Dickens's *Oliver Twist.*

A company background check revealed you are neither a self-starter nor a multitasker.

You've been accused of using banned substances to boost your overtime.

Your last three jobs were featured in the Bud Light "Real Men of Genius" radio commercials.

● ● ● ● ●

The last plant accident was probably no worse for your health than standing next to the sun for 10,000 years.

Your company physician was awarded a McDoctorate from Hamburger U.

• • • • •

Simon Cowell recommended you quit your day job even though you can't sing.

The company cafeteria is still serving canned tuna from the never-used Y2K survival bunker.

● ● ● ● ●

You neglected to change the oil in your car and wound up having to change the entire engine.

Your company benefits include
a dignified burial and group
discount on body armor.

• • • • •

**The CEO refers to himself as
Chief Entertainment Officer
and boosts productivity by
telling knock-knock jokes.**

201

You recently figured out that you work hard so that the company owners can play hard.

Your company provides a three-piece uniform: burlap sack, leather collar, and leg irons.

You live every day in fear that
management will replace
you with an electric fan.

Your NASA supervisor wasn't
kidding when he warned
your head might explode.

You got caught making dirty animations on company Post-it pads.

● ● ● ● ●

You've been a Motel Six Platinum Club member six years running.

● ● ● ● ●

Your Top Gun nickname is Douchebag.

One of your dental patients claims that you "checked her out" while she was under anesthesia.

• • • • •

Your company insurer is investigating why your "domestic partner" bit the mailman and might have fleas.

You don't get to clean up the roadkill until you've paid your dues.

• • • • •

The last three departments you worked in: Excess Capacity, Untrimmed Headcount, and Redundant Workforce.

Famous
Last Words

*It's been said that "no one's dying words were ever
'I wish I'd spent more time at the office.'"
What then were their dying words?*

"How were the receipts today at
Madison Square Garden?"
–*P. T. Barnum*

"All my possessions for a moment of time."
—Queen Elizabeth I

•

"I have offended God and mankind because my work did not reach the quality it should have."
—Leonardo da Vinci

•

"The bullet hasn't been made that can kill me!"
—Gangster Jack "Legs" Diamond,
just before being shot to death

•

"Die? I should say not, dear fellow. No Barrymore would allow such a conventional thing to happen to him."
—John Barrymore

"Good-bye, everybody!"
–Hart Crane, just before jumping overboard during a steamship voyage

•

"I should never have switched from Scotch to martinis."
–Humphrey Bogart

•

"That was the best ice-cream soda I ever tasted."
–Lou Costello

•

"Either that wallpaper goes, or I do."
–Oscar Wilde

"I wish I'd drunk more champagne."
–John Maynard Keynes

•

"Turn up the lights, I don't want
to go home in the dark."
*–O. Henry, quoting
a popular song*

•

"I hope I haven't bored you."
*–Elvis Presley, concluding his
last press conference*

•

"I'd rather be fishing."
*–Jimmy Glass, electrocuted
in Louisiana in 1987*

"Nonsense, they couldn't hit an elephant at this distance."
—*General John Sedgwick, refusing to hide behind a parapet during the Battle of the Wilderness*

•

"I have just had eighteen whiskeys in a row. I do believe that is a record."
—*Dylan Thomas*

•

"How about this for a headline for tomorrow's paper? French fries."
—*James French, electrocuted in Oklahoma in 1966*

Your new title: Vice President of Floor Security for Chicle and Other Resin-based (Used) Chewing Substances–Sales Aisles and Merchandising Areas.

The poster in the restroom reads: "Employees Need Not Wash Hands—No Amount of Scrubbing Will Remove the Filth."

The stock market crashed and you didn't have time to sell before it hit rock bottom.

• • • • •

Your Wells Fargo payroll is still delivered by stagecoach.

• • • • •

Sewer robots? There goes twelve years of training down the tubes.

213

You were forced to take an unpaid, eight-week "Drugs in the Workplace" training seminar after giving a co-worker two Midols.

● ● ● ● ●

You can't meet the minimum physical requirements for the fashion police.

You spend most of your waking hours making To Do lists.

• • • • •

Your idea of job security is putting Krazy Glue on your office chair.

• • • • •

Your start your day with the words "Gotta make the donuts."

215

Your briefcase is a steamer trunk.

● ● ● ● ●

The mere thought of trying to get airline reservations to Tahiti is overwhelming.

● ● ● ● ●

Your role model is a chicken running around without its head.

You're convinced that you're a character in Upton Sinclair's *The Jungle*.

You're constantly borrowing staplers from other co-workers' desks because you don't have time to go to the supply closet and get a new box of staples.

You're pretty sure that you personally served 1 billion of the 5 billion hamburgers served.

• • • • •

The closest you've come in the last year to taking a long, lingering bubble bath was scrubbing the baked-on gunk off the casserole dish.

218

Your exercise regimen consists
of cupping your palm under
a soap dispenser, pushing up
vigorously until you're convinced
that the soap dispenser is actually
empty, reaching over to the next
soap dispenser, and repeating
the process until you find one
that's got some soap in it.

You're seeing a chiropractor once a week because you attempted to leap over the maze of velvet ropes at the bank.

The knots in your garden hose earned you a Boy Scout badge.

You have an uncontrollable desire to alphabetize all the entries in this book.

You joined Overachievers Anonymous, but when you ran for president, tried to double the membership, and started selling franchises, they threw you out.

None of your socks match.

● ● ● ● ●

You've been telling yourself that you need a haircut–for the last six months.

● ● ● ● ●

Your personal library is really a roomful of books that you'll never find the time to read.

More than half the checks you've written this month have bounced.

● ● ● ● ●

Just the thought of going onto Travelocity, Orbitz, or Expedia gives you a migraine headache.

● ● ● ● ●

All your pencils have teeth marks.

To fit a spa treatment into your hectic schedule, you simply rolled down the windows while going through a car wash.

• • • • •

The family photo sitting on your desk isn't yours.

You just discovered that your name is misspelled on the business cards you've been handing out for the last three months.

● ● ● ● ●

Your passport expired— two years ago.

Your mother strapped you down for a high-speed ride on top of the Suburban to "test" the washability of high-tech thermal underwear.

● ● ● ● ●

Your spouse went on a second honeymoon without you.

226

You bought sneakers with Velcro straps so you don't have to waste time bending over to tie your shoelaces every time they come loose.

You get road rage just looking for your car keys.

• • • • •

When doing the wash, there's no need to separate the whites because they're all gray and pink.

Breakfast was a cup of coffee, lunch was Lipton's Cup-a-Soup, and dinner was a box of Good & Plenty.

● ● ● ● ●

On your birthday, you went into work early, stayed late, and completely forgot what day it was.

You wish you had a less stressful job—like spinning plates or juggling chain saws.

You're convinced that your co-workers are your extended family.

You don't care whether it rains on the weekend because you'll be working anyway.

You're convinced your life would be fine if each day lasted forty-eight hours.

Your last three days off: jury duty, traffic school, and 9/11.

● ● ● ● ●

You shave in the car.

● ● ● ● ●

Your kids refer to you as The Mighty Wallet.

232

You've held forth on how to pack a tuna lunch so the bread doesn't get soaked through.

● ● ● ● ●

Scott Adams sued you for posting too many *Dilbert* cartoons in your cubicle.

233

After FICA, Medicaid, and health insurance deductions, you have just enough money left in your paycheck to cover gas for the commute.

• • • • •

Your Scotch tape dispenser has been home to an empty plastic spool since the Mesozoic era.

Your front lawn looks like the Amazon rain forest.

● ● ● ● ●

If you put 5 percent of your earnings
away for the next forty years at
an average of 8 percent interest a
year, you'll accumulate just enough
money to pay for a nice funeral.

235

Your "call forwarding" bounces your incoming phone calls to six different call-forwarding services.

● ● ● ● ●

You don't recognize your kids at the dining room table.

You think heating up a can of Chef Boyardee ravioli takes too much time.

• • • • •

You've ironed a shirt while drinking a cup of coffee and shaving your legs.

You've been handed a subpoena while you were on the witness stand.

• • • • •

When the police tried to pull you over for speeding, you led them on a six-mile chase so you wouldn't be late to a meeting.

While sitting in the waiting room
at the doctor's office,
you do your taxes.

● ● ● ● ●

**Instead of taking a vacation,
you decided to remodel
the guest bathroom.**

You're convinced that when you get to heaven, you'll be judged by the number of items crossed off your Things To Do list.

You constantly forget to go to the bathroom.

240

Your co-workers talk about movies that you've never seen.

You accidentally left your résumé on the office photocopier.

You spend your entire day putting out small brush fires.

● ● ● ● ●

You bite your fingernails in your sleep.

● ● ● ● ●

Three new species of mold are growing inside your coffee mug.

242

It would be easier to buy a new set of dishes rather than scrub the old ones clean.

•　•　•　•　•

You've used a rolling pin to get more toothpaste out of the tube.

For every e-mail you delete,
you receive fifteen more.

• • • • •

Your nickname is Sisyphus.

• • • • •

Your calendar is booked solid—
right up until your funeral.

244

If you accidentally get on an elevator going the wrong direction, your world unravels.

• • • • •

No matter what time it is, you can't believe two hours just flew by.

You change checkout lanes at the supermarket at least three times in the futile hope of finding the shortest line and the fastest cashier.

If not for Hot Pockets, you'd starve to death.

• • • • •

Every day feels like you're about to land on Boardwalk with a hotel.

• • • • •

You're convinced that you are God's personal voodoo doll.

247

You put your mother on hold
and totally forgot about her.

● ● ● ● ●

You don't have time to relieve stress.

● ● ● ● ●

You dropped off your daughter
at soccer practice—wearing
a Girl Scout uniform.

One glance at your daily planner sends you into cardiac arrest.

• • • • •

You accidentally brushed your teeth with hemorrhoid ointment.

• • • • •

You left the groceries in the trunk of your car for a week.

249

You're reading this
book on a commuter
flight between New
York and Boston.